The Unspoken Rules of People Pleasers

Why Being "Nice" Is Costing You More Than You Realize

Shante Alexander, MA, PCC

CONTENTS

What This Book Is (and isn't)

This book isn't here to fix you. It's here to show you what you've been tolerating. If you've ever thought, "I don't know why I'm so tired — I'm doing what I'm supposed to be doing," this book is for you. Not because you're broken, but because you've been operating under rules you never consciously agreed to.

This isn't a guide on setting boundaries. It's not a checklist for refusing requests. It's not a productivity plan in disguise as self-care. Those will come later. This book focuses on recognition.

It's about recognizing the unspoken agreements that many people-pleasers and overgivers make with themselves long before they reach burnout — agreements that seem reasonable, responsible, and even virtuous. Until suddenly, they don't.

This book aims to uncover the beliefs many people quietly hold—those that justify overgiving, overfunctioning, and overextending, even when it's neither generous nor sustainable.

You might recognize yourself right away. You might feel uncomfortable. You might also feel strangely relieved. That's intentional. Because before change can happen, awareness must be honest. And honesty doesn't rush to a conclusion or demand immediate action.

This book won't pressure you to overhaul your life, confront everyone, or "finally put yourself first." That kind of urgency often adds another task to your to-do list. Instead, this book creates a gentler space — a place where you can speak honestly without feeling the need to apologize.

If you finish this book thinking, "Something has been off — and now I can see it," then it has fulfilled its purpose. The deeper work—the emotional cost, the identity shifts, the integration—belongs to another stage of the journey.

For now, this book encourages you to acknowledge what you have been feeling inside. And that alone can produce more change than you might realize.

When Niceness Becomes a Cover

"I'm so tired of always being nice."

Niceness didn't exhaust you. The role you built around it did. Many people see themselves in this statement. The irony is that most who relate aren't unkind, careless, or self-absorbed. They're exhausted from being needed. They're the ones who soften their tone, lower tension, and naturally make things easier for others. For many, over-giving started as a relational strength — a way to stay connected, considerate, and safe in unpredictable environments.

But being nice doesn't work in isolation. It reflects a deeper belief: that harmony must be maintained, comfort must be protected, and your needs can wait. Over time, doing it all becomes second nature.

It becomes your way of staying approachable, agreeable, and easy to understand. It also becomes how you prevent conflict, disappointment, or discomfort — not because you're hiding anything, but because you've learned that steadiness maintains stability. Over time, this can lead to a subtle internal split. On the outside, you appear accommodating. Inside, you may feel stretched, tired, or invisible.

This book isn't asking you to stop being nice. It's asking you to notice when niceness ceases to be a choice. It asks a gentler question:

What is your constant niceness and always-being-needed quietly costing you?

I Don't Know Who I Am If I'm Not Being Needed.

What This Looks Like in Real Life

I get up at five in the morning. Not because I want to — because the day will fall apart if I don't start early. I wake the kids, find their clothes, make sure they brush their teeth, pack their lunches, and put their shoes in the right spots. While the coffee brews, I check my phone. A work email came in last night. I decided to respond before anyone else was awake.

Someone can't find something. Someone needs a reminder. Someone needs help. I go through the morning without sitting down. On my way out, I check the list: drop-offs, meetings, errands, deadlines. Wait, did I eat anything? At work, people come to me because they know I'm dependable. I handle the things that "shouldn't take long." I step in when something is missing. I stay late because it's easier than explaining what's required.

By the time I get home, I'm already falling behind. Dinner needs preparing, homework needs checking, and baths need giving. My phone keeps buzzing—a question, a request, or a problem—and I answer all of them. When the house finally quiets down, I don't take a break. I scroll through my feed, plan for tomorrow, and catch up on unfinished tasks. By the time I lie down, I'm exhausted, but I've accomplished most of what was needed today. That feels like enough.

What This Belief Gives You

This belief gives you structure. Your day has a clear purpose. Your role is defined. Your value is obvious. When you're needed, you don't have to wonder where you belong. Your presence is justified by demand.

There's always something to respond to, fix, or manage. Movement keeps doubt at bay. Doing keeps discomfort from catching up. This rule works because it organizes your life around necessity—and necessity is predictable.

What This Belief Costs You

Over time, this rule favors function over identity. Your days are full—but not necessarily yours. You're not just staying busy—you're staying necessary. You're not choosing your life. You're maintaining your role. Your energy is spent reacting rather than making intentional choices.

You don't spend much time asking:

- What am I looking for?
- What do I enjoy?
- What motivates or excites me?

Those questions don't have deadlines. Rest feels earned only after everything else is taken care of—and nothing ever truly concludes. So even when the day ends, your sense of self doesn't arrive. Only fatigue does. You became who people needed—and forgot to check whether it was you.

Reasons Why This Pattern Continues

Because it keeps life moving, it prevents collapse. It keeps people satisfied and maintains order. Letting go of this rule would mean facing time without obligation—and when your identity is built around response, that space feels unfamiliar. You don't feel needed because you're valuable. You feel valuable because you're needed. So the rule stays, not because it's examined, but because it's efficient.

Recognition Point

I keep calling this responsibility, but it's actually how I know who I am.

How This Manifests as People-Pleasing

You stay available because being available feels like your role. You respond quickly, volunteer first, and step in before anyone needs to ask. You anticipate needs before they're spoken, smooth over tension, and keep things moving because predictability feels more stable than uncertainty. You rarely allow yourself to be unavailable—missed messages seem like missed relevance, and rest feels like slipping out of position. People-pleasing here isn't about generosity; it's about staying necessary enough to feel like you fit.

Lingering Questions

When everything relying on you is removed, what's left?

If I Don't Do It, It Won't Get Done Right.

What This Looks Like in Real Life

I'll check it quickly. That's all that's needed. I scan it once, then again. That part needs fixing. That won't work. The team missed something. If I leave it like this, it'll come back to me anyway. I should handle it. It'll be faster if I do it myself. I don't have time to explain. I don't want to follow up. I already know what needs adjustment.

I could ask someone else, but then I'd have to wait. I want to trust the process, but then I'd have to accept a result that's probably not quite right. I don't want to redo it later, so I'll do it now.

I identify issues before they become problems. I smooth things out. I make sure it works. No one notices the extra effort, and that's okay. What matters is that it's done right. Eventually, I believe, they will notice.

What This Belief Gives You

This belief boosts your confidence. When you're the one doing it, you understand the outcome. You don't have to wonder how it will turn out or worry about making mistakes. It also improves your efficiency. When you work alone, you move more quickly. You avoid back-and-forth and reduce delays. This belief keeps standards high and mistakes low. It protects you from embarrassment and ensures the work does not fall short. In situations where mistakes matter, this rule seems practical— even responsible.

What This Belief Costs You

Over time, this belief subtly causes overload. You take on more than your role requires—not because you're asked, but because you don't trust the outcome otherwise. You're not just helping—you're maintaining control. You're not stepping in because they can't do it. You're stepping in because you don't trust the outcome. Delegation is no longer necessary. Support systems become less effective. Working together seems risky.

You carry the weight of execution and the pressure of results. And while tasks are completed, the pressure never is.

In the process, you become increasingly lonely. This rule also limits growth around you. Others don't improve because there's no room to try. You remain essential—and over time, that can become draining.

Reasons Why This Pattern Continues

Because it produces results, things get done. Mistakes are avoided. Standards stay high. Letting go of this rule means accepting imperfection—and trusting outcomes you can't fully control. When your sense of safety depends on competence, that feels risky. So, the rule stays. Not because it's fair— but because it works.

Recognition Point

I don't trust things to be okay unless I'm the one in charge of handling them.

    The Unspoken Rules of People Pleasers

How This Manifests as People-Pleasing

You overextend yourself to avoid disappointment. You take on tasks not because others can't do them, but because fixing their mistakes feels more uncomfortable than doing it yourself. You quietly double-check and redo their work to maintain stability. People-pleasing here isn't just about saying yes—it's about never letting go.

Lingering Questions

When everything that depends on you is gone, what remains?

I Have to Earn My Seat at the Table.

What This Looks Like in Real Life

Them: "Can someone lead this project?"

Me: "I've already started it."

Them: "We don't have to stay late; the project can wait till tomorrow."

Me: "I'm almost finished."

Them: "Oh, we're still brainstorming."

Me: "I brought a draft in case it helps."

Them: "Great! Can you send a follow-up?"

Me: "It's already in your inbox."

Them: "Thanks—this really helps."

No one tells me I don't belong here, but I feel the room watching to see if I'll prove it. So, I stay prepared. I remain helpful. I stay ahead. I pay attention to tone. I observe faces. I choose my words carefully.

I don't interrupt. I don't take risks. I don't take up space unless I've earned it twice. When I speak, I am precise and beyond question.

I stay alert—because attention shifts quickly. And I've learned that being visible isn't the same as being valued.

What This Belief Gives You

At first, it grants you access. You don't assume belonging — you earn it. You build credibility through preparation, precision, and performance. If you're useful, you're harder to dismiss; if you're competent, you're harder to overlook. It also provides direction—there's always something to improve, anticipate, or strengthen.

You understand the rules: stay prepared, stay sharp, stay valuable. And in environments where people like you have been questioned or excluded, this belief feels more like a strategy than insecurity. It's how you navigate rooms that weren't built with you in mind.

What This Belief Costs You

Eventually, this pattern diminishes your sense of peace. You don't walk into rooms relaxed—you enter scanning for signs, monitoring tone, and watching how you're perceived. Your confidence becomes conditional; when you contribute, you feel steady, and when you don't, doubt floods in. You present the most polished version of yourself because authenticity feels risky when belonging has to be earned. Beneath it all is the quiet fear that if you stop proving your worth, you could be dismissed. So you keep earning—even when no one asks you to.

Reasons Why This Pattern Continues

Because it feels protective, earning your seat creates the illusion of control. If you prepare, perform, and contribute enough, you can avoid exclusion. But you're not just earning your seat. You're proving you deserve to be in the room. In environments where belonging is conditional and visibility must be justified, proving your value becomes a survival skill—especially for women and marginalized professionals. So the rule remains, not because it's true, but because it feels safer than trusting your presence alone. You enter rooms ready to demonstrate your value, staying attentive and useful, and monitoring how you're perceived before you relax. Belonging doesn't feel automatic; it feels conditional.

Recognition Point

I can't relax in a room—I'm too busy trying to prove I belong there.

How This Manifests as People-Pleasing

You perform to belong. You enter rooms ready to prove your worth because visibility feels safer than staying in the background. Overworking becomes a tactic, and competence serves as armor. You observe how others see you, adjust your space, and add value before settling in. People-pleasing here isn't about seeking approval; it's about securing your position before it's challenged.

Lingering Questions

Who would you be in the room if you didn't feel the need to prove you belong there?

I Don't Want to Disappoint Them.

What This Looks Like in Real Life

I'm already exhausted, and the weekend hasn't even started. It's been a tough week. I haven't been feeling well, but I kept pushing through because I had too much to do. Now, tomorrow is the big family dinner at my in-laws.

I'm supposed to bring the pot roast. Everyone looks forward to it every month. If it's not there…

I consider saying something—admitting I can't do it this time. But then I picture their expressions—some annoyed, others surprised, most just disappointed. So I start planning anyway. I tell myself it's just one more thing. I can rest later. It's simply easier to push through now than to have to apologize and explain later.

Besides, it's better to arrive tired than to be remembered as the person who didn't show up and left everyone hungry.

What This Belief Gives You

What this reinforces is the belief that connection comes through consistency. When you meet expectations, relationships stay smooth. You remain integrated without pushing your limits. It also provides you with relational safety. By being dependable, you avoid awkward conversations, disappointment, or the need to adjust. You don't have to worry about how others might respond to your honesty. Being nice and needed becomes a way to maintain harmony—quietly, predictably, reliably.

What This Belief Costs You

This pattern erodes your peace of mind. You make decisions based on what others might think rather than what you can genuinely offer. You stay mentally busy managing perceptions before they even develop. It also diminishes your confidence. When every situation feels like one that requires approval, your sense of worth becomes unstable. If you perform well, you feel secure. If not, self-doubt creeps in. And it costs you authenticity. You don't present yourself as a whole person with limits and needs. Instead, you show up as the version of yourself least likely to disappoint. You're not choosing peace—you're avoiding reaction. You're not maintaining harmony. You're managing perception.

Reasons Why This Pattern Continues

Because it protects the connection, you've learned that disappointment changes how people respond, and avoiding it feels easier than managing the reactions that follow. In environments where being agreeable was rewarded and boundaries created friction, this belief becomes familiar. So, the rule stays—not because anyone demands it, but because disappointing others reliably complicates things.

Recognition Point

I keep calling it being considerate, but I'm genuinely afraid of what might happen if I stop.

How This Manifests as People-Pleasing

This is where giving turns into self-neglect. You prioritize others' comfort over your own boundaries and call it "easy to deal with." You say yes to avoid reactions you don't want to manage. Showing up becomes a shield—keeping things smooth, predictable, and free of tension. You monitor how you're perceived, adjust your presence, and stay agreeable so no one has to recalibrate around you. People-pleasing here isn't kindness; it's a way to manage the dynamics around you.

Lingering Questions

What if disappointment never felt like a threat to belonging?

I Feel Guilty When I'm Not Doing Something.

What This Looks Like in Real Life

I finally sit down—and I don't relax. The house is quiet. Nothing is pulling at me urgently. There's a rare opening in the day. But instead of feeling relief, I feel uneasy.

I check my phone. No messages. No fires. My mind starts scanning. There's laundry I could fold, an email I could reply to, or something I could get ready for tomorrow.

Sitting still feels wrong, unproductive, and wasteful. I tell myself I'll rest in a minute—after I do just one more thing. When I stop moving, guilt sneaks in, like I'm getting away with something or being lazy.

So, I get up. Not because I have to — but because doing something feels more responsible than just sitting still.

What This Belief Gives You

At first, this gives you moral reassurance. When you're doing something, you feel justified. Your time appears accounted for. Activity becomes evidence that you're responsible, involved, and contributing. You don't need to wonder if you're doing enough—because you're always doing something. This belief also leads to emotional avoidance. Movement pushes discomfort away. Stillness prevents questions you'd rather avoid from arising. Doing keeps you calm and in control.

What This Belief Costs You

Over time, this reinforces the idea that you lose rest without any penalty. You don't see downtime as neutral; instead, you view it as needing justification. Your body might stop, but your mind doesn't. It also demands your attention. Moments that could be relaxing feel tense. Silence seems unproductive. Comfort feels strange. And it costs you self-compassion. You judge your progress by output. You're not resting—you're waiting to feel allowed to stop. You don't feel tired. You feel unproductive. If you're not creating, you feel behind—even when nothing is actually expected of you.

Reasons Why This Pattern Continues

Guilt is wired as a motivator. You've learned that staying busy aligns you with expectations—spoken or unspoken. That doing equals value, and rest must be earned. This belief often takes root in environments where productivity is praised over presence and where slowing down means falling behind. So, the pattern continues. Not because guilt is helpful—but because it reliably keeps you moving.

Recognition Point

When I cease doing, I don't feel free—I feel wrong.

How This Manifests as People-Pleasing

This is how kindness can turn into constant self-monitoring. You stay busy to avoid seeming lazy, unmotivated, or ungrateful. You keep working so no one questions your effort—even when no one is truly paying attention. People-pleasing isn't always about agreeing with others. Sometimes, it means never permission yourself to stop.

Lingering Questions

What would rest feel like if it didn't need justification?

If I Slow Down, I'll Fall Behind.

What This Looks Like in Real Life

My friend invites me to the pottery class she's been hyping up. I want to go. I really do. But I look at my week and think, I can't afford to slow down. If I take a night off, I'll lose momentum. If I skip a task, I'll fall behind. If I rest, I'll pay for it later.

Then I see someone I know sharing photos from a weekend trip. Another friend just picked up a new hobby. Someone else is dating again—already on their third match this month. Everyone seems to be moving forward. Building lives. Trying new things and meeting new people.

I'm not sure how they make space for it. I only know I can't. So, I stay busy. I keep my schedule packed. I keep choosing productivity over leisure. I keep telling myself I'll make room for life later because slowing down doesn't feel like truly living. It feels like losing ground.

What This Belief Gives You

This pattern creates a purposeful sense of urgency. Scarcity sharpens your focus, keeping you attentive. It convinces you that effort equals protection. You feel motivated—not because you're inspired, but because you believe there's no time, space, or opportunity to waste. This belief also fuels your competitiveness. As long as you keep moving, you think you're still in the race. You haven't fallen behind or been replaced. Scarcity becomes ambition—and it works until it doesn't.

What This Belief Costs You

Eventually, this pattern weakens your discernment. When everything feels urgent, you can't evaluate things properly. You confuse movement with progress, yet you're not moving forward—you're just afraid of falling behind. It also erodes your trust. You don't believe opportunities can wait. You don't trust there will be space for you if you step back. You don't trust that your worth isn't tied to constant climbing. What once served survival now costs you peace because scarcity never settles. There's always someone faster. Always something more. So you keep chasing—not fulfillment, but status.

Reasons Why This Pattern Continues

Because scarcity fosters compliance. When you believe there's not enough to go around, slowing down feels irresponsible. This idea is reinforced by cultures of comparison, metrics, visibility, and competition—where attention and opportunity seem limited and fleeting. As a result, the pattern persists. Not because speed is sustainable— but because scarcity convinces you it's necessary.

Recognition Point

I'm not entirely motivated by growth — I'm afraid of losing my role.

How This Manifests as People-Pleasing

This is people-pleasing under pressure. You stay visible, available, and responsive so you don't get overlooked. You keep pace so no one questions your relevance or commitment. Niceness here looks like compliance with urgency—agreeing to a system that treats scarcity as reality.

Lingering Questions

What would slow down if you stopped believing opportunity was about to end?

This Is Just Who I Am.

What This Looks Like in Real Life

Them: "Why do you always step in? You never let anything drop."

I shrug and say, "This is just who I am. It's how I've always been."

I say it without thinking. I'm the dependable one. The responsible one. The one who takes care of everything. I no longer question it.

I use it to explain myself, justify my choices, and make sense of my reactions. I don't pause to ask whether I chose this or if it was chosen for me. It feels final, like a fact I shouldn't question. Trying to picture myself without these traits feels strange—almost dishonest. It's like I'd be pretending and abandoning something essential.

So, I tell myself again, this is just who I am.

What This Belief Gives You

At first, it gives you certainty. It removes the need to struggle with change or ambiguity. It eliminates curiosity about who you'd be without these patterns. Labeling adaptation as identity creates stability. It turns behavior into character. It makes long-practiced roles feel real. It also offers relief. If this is just who you are, there's nothing to examine or question. The story feels complete.

What This Belief Costs You

It restricts your options. When adaptation becomes part of your identity, flexibility disappears. Growth feels like a betrayal rather than progress. It also undermines your self-trust. You stop asking whether your patterns still serve you. You assume they're fixed—even when they drain you. And it limits what you can achieve. Parts of you that never had space to grow remain unexplored—not because they don't exist, but because the role you learned to play takes up all the air.

Reasons Why This Pattern Continues

Because identity feels more grounded than uncertainty, recognizing that these patterns were adaptive—not essential—means acknowledging how much of you was shaped by pressure. You didn't choose this role. You adapted to it, and that realization brings grief. So the mind settles on a simpler explanation: This is just who I am. It protects you from revisiting the forces that made you who you are. It shields you from the discomfort of change. The belief persists because it sidesteps the question.

Recognition Point

I stopped dreaming when I stopped believing I could be anything else.

How This Manifests as People-Pleasing

This is where people-pleasing becomes integrated into your self-identity. You don't merely behave in an accommodating manner—you begin to see yourself as easygoing, helpful, and low-maintenance. Over-functioning transforms from a strategy to a core aspect of your personality. When constantly adapting becomes part of who you are, stepping out of that role can feel like losing your sense of self.

Lingering Questions

Who could you become if you didn't restrict yourself to just this version of you?

When Generosity Turns Transactional

By now, you might understand why niceness and always being needed feel so overwhelming. Not because you're unkind. Not because you want to be mean. But because the rules you've been living by have been guiding you — often without your approval. People may have asked you:

- Why do you feel responsible for everything and everyone?
- Why didn't you reach out for help?
- Why did you say yes if you didn't want to?

Maybe you didn't have the words then. But you do now. You can see how your beliefs shaped your choices. How your constant availability became a role you played, how exhaustion stemmed from patterns that no longer felt optional. You're not tired of being kind. You're tired of being consumed. You're tired of the version of giving that requires self-abandonment. And now you can finally understand why. When your identity is built on being needed, exhaustion becomes inevitable.

When the Pattern Reveals Itself

Nothing dramatic might happen here. You might not suddenly see your whole life differently. There may not be an immediate breakthrough, collapse, or revelation. Instead, recognition could be the only thing that occurs. You can start to notice that the rules aren't standalone; they mirror and reinforce each other. They create a rhythm you've been following for years. If more than one rule feels familiar, that's important. It shows this isn't just about a single habit; it's a pattern. Once you recognize the pattern, it's hard to unsee it.

When Awareness Meets Habit

Even after recognizing it, the pattern continues. You notice it as it happens, sometimes immediately, sometimes halfway through a familiar yes. You catch yourself people-pleasing again.

Overextending, smoothing things over, and then feeling the shame creep in and the uncomfortable thought: " I understand this now. Why am I still doing it? What's wrong with me?" Awareness doesn't undo conditioning; it just shines a light on it. And when the lights are on, it can feel worse — not better — to see yourself repeat something you now recognize.

This is the part no one warns you about. Recognition doesn't mean mastery. Seeing the pattern doesn't imply you can stop it right away. This moment isn't evidence that clarity failed. It shows that the behavior was serving you long before you had words for it.

Why This Finally Makes Sense

Being a giver isn't neutral because giving always has a purpose, even when we don't realize it. For many people-pleasers, generosity becomes a strategy—one that maintains connection, manages perception, prevents conflict, and secures a sense of worth. Niceness and always being needed can feel like proof that you matter, that you belong, that you're safe. Over time, this becomes a form of self-protection rather than simple kindness. And once you see that your helpfulness has been carrying the weight of identity, safety, and acceptance, the entire pattern finally comes into focus. This is the moment when the rules you've lived by start to make sense—and the moment you can begin choosing new ones.

Seeing Your Past Through a Clearer Lens

Looking back, the rules make sense. They weren't random. They weren't flaws. They were responses. Each one helped you stay connected, capable, or included. Each one solved a problem at the time. That doesn't make them harmless. But it does make them understandable. And that distinction matters.

Because shame loosens its grip when behavior finally makes sense, and once it makes sense, you stop asking, "What's wrong with me?" and start asking, "What was I protecting?" That question changes everything.

Before You Decide What Happens Next

You don't need to make any decisions right now. You don't need to change or fix yourself. You don't need a plan. Allow recognition to settle naturally. Clarity comes in its own time. Pushing for the next step too soon can turn insight into performance. Trust your pace. And when you're ready — even quietly ready — there is a place to move forward.

The Emotional Cost of Clarity™

At some point, naming the pattern isn't enough.

You begin to wonder:

- Why does this still feel so heavy?
- Why does clarity hurt just as much as it helps?
- Why does seeing it make me anxious instead of calm?

You don't need to fix this yet. But you won't be able to unsee it.

The Emotional Cost of Clarity™ exists for that reason. It doesn't introduce new rules. It examines what living by them has cost you — emotionally, relationally, professionally.

This eBook helps you identify the pattern. That book explores its impact deeply and what can happen when you begin to challenge it.

If this stirred something deeper than relief, that's where the work goes on.

Visit <u>www.shantealexander.com</u> to continue the journey to clarity.

Continue the Journey

If the patterns in this book felt familiar, you're not imagining it.

Many high achievers and people-pleasers quietly build lives that look successful on the outside — while feeling exhausted underneath.

This book helps you see the pattern. *The Emotional Cost of Clarity*™ shows you what it's been costing you. It explores the deeper identity patterns behind burnout, over-functioning, and the pressure to prove your value.

You can continue the journey here: Scan the QR code below to begin.